Favorite ROSES Coloring Book

Ilil Arbel

Dover Publications, Inc.   New York

Publisher's Note

The roses, in all their splendid diversity, are the world's best known and most loved flowers. Cultivated since antiquity, they have developed an astounding variety of form, color, scent and behavior. All of the thousands of rose varieties can be crossbred, for all belong to the same genus, *Rosa*. This fact has allowed for an infinite range of possible characteristics for cultivators to work with. In addition, modern biotechnological advances are now being brought to bear on the development of new rose types, unusual colorations and improved characteristics (e.g., length of blooming season).

Given all the clamor surrounding contemporary additions to the catalog of roses, with their unprecedented colors and forms, one should not overlook the venerable old historic garden roses, including Rosa Mundi, Austrian Copper and Great Maiden's Blush. These flowers have acquired a certain historical patina, and possess charms that have proven durable. A representative selection of these old roses is contained within the pages of this book.

Roses now come in a wide assortment of "applications": ground cover, climbing, miniature and shrub. This book should help to indicate some of the different ways in which roses can be deployed. At the end of the book is a brief glossary that describes the rose types found in this book.

Copyright © 1988 by Dover Publications, Inc.
All rights reserved under Pan American and International Copyright Conventions.

Published in Canada by General Publishing Company, Ltd., 30 Lesmill Road, Don Mills, Toronto, Ontario.

Favorite Roses Coloring Book is a new work, first published by Dover Publications, Inc., in 1988.

DOVER *Pictorial Archive* SERIES

International Standard Book Number: 0-486-25845-9

Manufactured in the United States of America
Dover Publications, Inc., 31 East 2nd Street, Mineola, N.Y. 11501

1. **America** (Climber)

Moderately tall climber, with medium-green, leathery foliage.
Flowers are coral pink, double, 4″–5″, with spicy fragrance.
Blooms resemble Hybrid Teas.

2. **Arizona** (Grandiflora)

Tall bush, with bronze-green foliage. Flowers are double, 4.5″, and have a strong Tea fragrance. Color is an unusual golden bronze.

3. **Bahia** (Floribunda)

An upright plant with bronze, glossy foliage. The flowers are double, 2.5″–4″, bright orange. Fragrance is light and spicy.

4. **Blaze** (Climber)

Fast-growing climber with medium-green, leathery leaves.
Blooms in large clusters. Flowers are scarlet, semi-double,
2″–3″, with slight fragrance.

5. **Brandy** (Hybrid Tea)

Brandy is a tall, bushy plant, with large, semi-glossy foliage. Flowers are double, 4″–5″, borne singly on long stems. Color is golden apricot. Brandy has a mild Tea fragrance. Introduced 1982.

6. Cecile Brunner (Polyantha)

Short, upright bush with tiny, dark, glossy foliage. Flowers are double, 1″–5″, blooming in clusters. Color is a light yellowish pink. The fragrance is delicate, though sweet and distinctive. Introduced in 1881 (France), a cross between a Polyantha and a Tea.

7. **Charisma** (Floribunda)

Compact, bushy plant, with leathery foliage. Flowers are double, 2.5″–3″, blooming singly and in clusters. Color is scarlet and yellow, with the red intensifying with age. Fragrance is slight.

8. Cherry Vanilla (Grandiflora)

Upright, tall plant with dark, semi-glossy foliage. Flowers are double, 4.5″, with moderate Tea fragrance. Color is yellow edged with dark pink.

9. **China Doll** (Polyantha)

Very small bush, low-growing, with leathery foliage. The flowers are double, 1″–2″, covering the plant in masses. Color is rose pink, with yellow base, and the fragrance is slight.

10. **Cinderella** (Miniature)

Small plant, 12″–15″, with glossy foliage. Flowers are double,
¾″–1″, blooming profusely. Color is light pink, fading to white.
Fragrance is spicy.

11. Color Magic (Hybrid Tea)

A medium-height bush, with large, dark and glossy foliage. Flowers are double, 6″–7″, borne singly on long stems. Color is ivory to deep rose, darkening with age. Color Magic has a light, pleasant fragrance.

12. **Communis, Common Moss** (Moss)

Upright, tall plant, with rough, dark green foliage. Flowers are very double, 2″–3″. Buds, stems and sepals are covered with reddish "moss," sticky and pine-scented. The flowers are extremely fragrant. Dates from before 1700 (France).

13. **Double Delight** (Hybrid Tea)

Considered an excellent cut flower, Double Delight is a medium-height, spreading plant with dark, glossy foliage. Flowers are double, 5.5″–6″, blooming in profusion. Color is creamy white at the center to red on the edges, with the amount of red increasing with age or with hot weather. Fragrance is moderate. Introduced 1977 (U.S.A.).

14. **Duchesse de Brabant** (Tea)

Upright, though spreading, bush with glossy foliage. Flowers are
very double, 2″–3″. Color is soft, clear rosy pink. Fragrance is
strong. Dates from 1857 (France).

15. **Europeana** (Floribunda)

Small, bushy plant, with red and green foliage. Flowers are dark crimson, double, about 3″. Blooms in many heavy clusters.

16. **First Edition** (Floribunda)

Medium-height bush with olive-green, leathery foliage. Flowers are semi-double, 2.5″, blooming singly and in clusters. Color is coral orange, darkening in cool climates. Fragrance is slight.

17. First Prize (Hybrid Tea)

Particularly successful exhibition rose, First Prize is a medium-height, spreading plant, with dark, leathery, tapered foliage. Flowers are double, about 6″, borne on long stems. Color is rose pink, with ivory center. The flowers have a light, "old rose" fragrance.

18. **Garden Party** (Hybrid Tea)

Medium-height, bushy plant, with abundant, semi-glossy, dark green foliage. Flowers are double, 4″–5″, with a color combination of pale yellow fading to white and light pink edges. Fragrance is slight.

19. **Gold Coin** (Miniature)

Very compact, low-growing plant, 8″–12″ tall, with dark, leathery foliage. Flowers are double, about 1.5″, shaped like Hybrid Tea, and fragrant. Color is buttercup yellow.

20. **Golden Showers** (Climber)

Medium-height climber with dark, glossy foliage. Flowers are a rich medium yellow (which turns rapidly to a more creamy color), double, 3.5"–4", moderately fragrant. Introduced in 1956 (U.S.A.).

21. **Great Maiden's Blush** (Alba)

Tall bush, with blue-greenish-gray foliage. Flowers are very double (up to 200 petals), 2″–3″, with a cultivated scent. Color is very light pink. This rose dates from at least the 1400's (Europe).

22. **Hermosa** (China)

Small bush, with gray-green, abundant but small leaves. Flowers
are double, 1″–3″, blooming in clusters. Color is average pink,
and the fragrance is moderate. Introduced in 1840 (France).

23. **Holy Toledo** (Miniature)

Large for a miniature, about 20″, with deep green, glossy foliage.
Flowers are about 2″, with slight fragrance. Color is orange, with
yellow center and reverse. Introduced in 1978.

24. **John S. Armstrong**
(Grandiflora)

Medium-sized bush with deep
green foliage. Flowers are 3.5″–4″,
free-blooming. Color is deep
yellow, but the buds are a darker
orange red.

25. **La Reine Victoria** (Bourbon)

Narrow, tall plant, with smooth, medium-green foliage. Flowers are double, 1.5″–2.5″, delicately fragrant. Color is medium pink with an admixture of moderate purple. Introduced 1872 (France).

26. **Love** (Grandiflora)

Full, bushy plant, with thick, medium-green foliage. Flowers are double, 3.5″, and have a spicy fragrance. Color is scarlet with white reverse.

27. **Maréchal Niel** (Noisette)

Vigorous climber, with somber reddish-green foliage. Flowers are double, 2″–3″, golden yellow, and highly fragrant. Developed in 1864 (France) from a lineage of Noisettes.

28. **Mister Lincoln** (Hybrid Tea)

Medium-height, bushy plant, with dark, leathery foliage. Flowers are double, 4″–7″, on long stems. Flowers are a deep, dark red and highly fragrant. Winner of the most show awards among roses. Introduced 1964 (U.S.A.).

29. **New Dawn** (Climber)

Tall climber, with dark, glossy foliage. Flowers are light pink, semi-double, 2″–3″, very fragrant. This sport was discovered in 1930 (U.S.A.), arising from the variety Dr. Van Fleet.

30. **Paradise** (Hybrid Tea)

Short, bushy plant with semi-glossy, deep green foliage. Flowers are semi-double, up to 5″. Color is lavender edged with red. It is considered a good cut flower. Introduced 1979.

31. **Peace** (Hybrid Tea)

Definitely the most famous of the Hybrid
Teas, if not all roses, Peace is a strong, bushy
plant, with dark, glossy leaves. Flowers are
very double (up to 45 petals), 5″–6″. Color
is a rich buttery yellow with pink (changing
to red) edges, though Peace can change its
hue overnight! Fragrance is subtle. Introduced in 1945 (France).

32. **Pink Parfait** (Grandiflora)

Bushy plant with light green foliage. Flowers are double, 3.5",
blooming singly and in clusters. They are medium to light pink
and have light fragrance.

33. **Prominent** (Grandiflora)

Medium-size bush with glossy foliage. Flowers are double, 3″, borne singly and in clusters. Color is a strong, bright orange, and fragrance is light and pleasant.

34. *Rosa eglanteria*, Sweet Briar Rose (species rose)

Tall, vigorous shrub, with small, scented foliage and bright red
oval hips (fruit). Flowers are single, 1.5″–2″, borne in clusters.
Color is clear pink. Fragrance is true rose, light and sweet. This
truly ancient rose originated in Europe many hundreds of years
ago.

35. ***Rosa foetida bicolor***, **Austrian Copper** (species
rose)

Tall plant with dark green foliage and bright red hips. Flowers
are 2″–2.5″, single, borne in sprays along the branches. Color is
orange copper, with a more yellow center. The *bicolor* is a sport
from the yellow *R. foetida* but has a much less "fetid" fragrance.
Dates from before the 1500's (Asia).

36. **Rosa Mundi** (Gallica)

Scientifically, this variety is *Rosa gallica versicolor*, a sport of *Rosa gallica officinalis* (The Apothecary's Rose, Red Rose of Lancaster) that first occurred in the remote past. Low, spreading plant with dark green, rough foliage. Flowers are 2″–3″, semi-double, striped red, pink and white. Fragrance is moderate though tenacious.

37. **Rose Parade** (Floribunda)

Compact, bushy plant, with dark green, glossy foliage. Flowers are double, about 3.5″, coral pink, blooming in clusters. Fragrance is strong.

38. Royal Highness (Hybrid Tea)

Medium-height, bushy plant, with deep green, leathery foliage.
Flowers are double, 5″–5.5″, light pink. Fragrance is heavy Tea.

39. Royal Sunset (Climber)

Strong climber, with coppery-green foliage.
Flowers are double, about 4.5″, apricot to
peach, slightly fragrant.

40. **Starina** (Miniature)

Moderately small for a miniature, 15″–18″ tall, with small, glossy foliage. Flowers are double, 1.5″–2″, borne in clusters. Color is orange scarlet. Starina has little or no fragrance.

41. Sundowner (Grandiflora)

Tall plant, with dark green, glossy foliage. Flowers are double, 3.5″–4″, blooming singly or in clusters but always in profusion. Color is golden orange, and fragrance is heavy.

42. **The Fairy** (Polyantha)

Compact, low, spreading plant with dark, fern-like foliage. Flowers are about 1.5″, blooming profusely in large clusters. Color is medium pink, and fragrance is slight. Developed in 1932 (U.K.).

43. **Tropicana** (Hybrid Tea)

Medium-height, spreading plant, with dark,
glossy foliage. Flowers are double, 4″–5″,
borne on long stems. Color is a strong orange
red that never fades or changes, even in the
sun. Fragrance is strong and fruity.

44. **Tuscany Superb** (Gallica)

Strong, compact plant with heavy, dark green foliage. Flowers
are semi-double, 4″–5″, blooming singly and in clusters. Petals
are velvety with a rich dark crimson coloration. Fragrance is
fairly strong. Developed in 1848 (U.K.) from the smaller
Tuscany, which originated in the Renaissance.

45. **York and Lancaster** (Damask)

Bushy, even somewhat unkempt, plant, with gray-green, rough foliage. Flowers are semi-double, 2.5″–3″, sometimes white, sometimes pink, or with differently colored petals. Fragrance is moderate for a Damask.

Glossary

Alba. The Albas have been cultivated since ancient times. They are tall with double, white, fragrant flowers.

Bourbon. Bourbons are a cross between China and Damask roses. They have semi-double or double blooms in shades of white, pink, red and purple.

China. Introduced from China during the eighteenth century. They are medium-sized plants with small flowers, produced in clusters, in shades of pink.

Climbers, Climbing Roses. Roses that can be induced to grow upon trellises, walls or pillars, or up into the branches of trees. These are divided into large-flowered climbers, with rigid, thick stems, and ramblers, with flexible stems.

Damask. The Damasks are native to the eastern Mediterranean, brought to Europe by the Crusaders. The Damasks have extremely strong fragrance and semi-double or double flowers in various shades of pink.

Double. Describes a type of flower consisting of manifold sets of petals, typically occurring in cultivated roses. Semi-double refers to a state intermediate between single and double, retaining the prominent pollen-coated stamens of the single flower.

Floribunda. A modern rose type, a cross between Hybrid Tea and Polyantha. Combines the qualities of both parents.

Gallica. Compact plants, the Gallicas have been cultivated since the Middle Ages. Their flowers range from single through double, in pink through red shades.

Grandiflora. A modern rose type, a cross between Hybrid Tea and Floribunda. 3–6-foot-tall plants, combining the good qualities of both parents to perfection—long stems, large flowers borne either singly or in clusters. Blooms are double. They do not have the wonderful fragrance of the Tea roses, though.

Hybrid Tea. These are the most popular roses in cultivation. Their long and narrow buds, on long stems, open to large fragrant flowers in a vast array of colors. Developed from the Teas.

Miniature Roses. 6–18 inches tall, probably descended from *Rosa chinensis minima*, with hundreds of different varieties: climbers, bushes, Mosses, etc., in every color and shape.

Moss. The Mosses have been cultivated since the 1600's, having arisen as sports from Centifolia (developed by hybridizing Hollanders in the 1500's). Like Centifolia, the Mosses have enormous blooms, are very double and fragrant, in whites, purples and reds, but have a green or reddish-brown mosslike growth covering their stems and sepals.

Noisette. The Noisettes are a cross between the Musk Rose and a China rose, first developed in the late 1700's, often climbers with the same fragrance and colors as Tea.

Old Garden Roses. These are roses that were introduced before 1867, the year the first Hybrid Tea was created (La France). They include Gallica, Damask, Alba, Centifolia, Moss, China, Bourbon, Portland, Noisette, Tea and Hybrid Perpetual roses. Roses developed after 1867 are termed "modern."

Polyantha. Polyanthas are the result of a cross between *Rosa multiflora* and a hybrid China, dating from the 1870's. They are low plants, with clusters of small flowers (single to double) in all Tea shades, but with R. *multiflora*'s long leaves.

Single. The simplest rose flowers, consisting of one set of five petals.

Species Roses. Species roses are those growing naturally in the wild. All roses are descended from them. They hybridize easily with the help of bees and other insects. These roses usually have single or semi-double blooms. Though delicate in appearance, they are quite hardy and easy to cultivate in a garden.

Tea. Tea roses were imported from China in the early 1800's. Their flowers are semi-double to double in shades of pink, white and yellow, with a distinctive, strong fragrance. These roses have no real connection with tea except that they arrived with the tea trade.